Scholastic Success With

GRAMMAR

WORKBOOK

GRADE 1

SCHOLASTIC
PROFESSIONAL BOOKS

New York • Toronto • London • Auckland • Sydney • Mexico City
New Delhi • Hong Kong • Buenos Aires

About the Book

"Nothing Succeeds Like Success."
–Alexandre Dumas the Elder, 1854

And no other resource boosts kids' grammar skills like *Scholastic Success With Grammar*! For classroom or at-home use, this exciting series for kids in grades 1 through 6 provides invaluable reinforcement and practice in grammar topics such as:

- sentence types
- parts of speech
- common and proper nouns
- sentence structure
- contractions
- verb tenses
- subject-verb agreement
- punctuation
- capitalization
  and more!

Each 64-page book contains loads of clever practice pages to keep kids challenged and excited as they strengthen the grammar skills they need to read and write well.

You'll also find lots of assessment sheets that give kids realistic practice in taking standardized tests – and help you see their progress!

What makes Scholastic Success With Grammar so solid?

Each practice page in the series reinforces a specific, age-appropriate skill as outlined in one or more of the following standardized tests:

- Iowa Tests of Basic Skills
- California Tests of Basic Skills
- California Achievement Test
- Metropolitan Achievement Test
- Stanford Achievement Test

Take the lead and help kids succeed with *Scholastic Success With Grammar*. Parents and teachers agree: No one helps kids succeed like Scholastic.

Table of Contents

ISBN: 0-439-43398-3

Name

Capitalize First Word

A sentence always begins with a capital letter.

 Draw a line under the first letter in each sentence.
Read each sentence to a friend.

1 The cat sat on a rat. **2** The rat sat on a hat.

3 The hat is on the dog. **4** The dog is on a mat.

Capitalize First Word

A sentence always begins with a capital letter.

▶ Copy each sentence correctly on the line.

1 the cat sat.

2 the dog sat.

3 i see the cat.

4 i can see.

Capitalize First Word

▶ Read each sentence. Then fill in the circle next to the word with the capital letter that begins the sentence.

1 The cat is in the van.

- ◯ cat
- ◯ The

2 My dog can run.

- ◯ My
- ◯ dog

3 Jan can hop.

- ◯ Jan
- ◯ hop

4 I like ham.

- ◯ ham
- ◯ I

5 Ants like jam.

- ◯ jam
- ◯ Ants

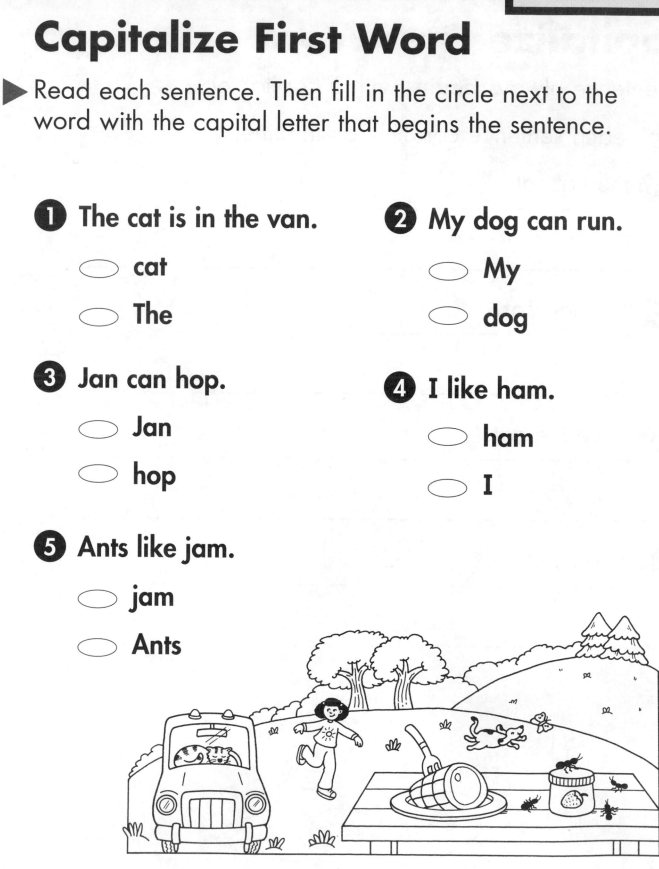

Periods

A telling sentence ends with a period.

 Circle the period at the end of each sentence.

1 I see Jan.

2 I go with Jan.

3 We see Dan.

4 I go with Dan and Jan.

▶ Draw a line under the last word in each sentence. Add a period to each sentence.

5 We go to school

6 We like school

Periods

A telling sentence ends with a period.

▶ Write a period where it belongs in each sentence. Read the sentences to a friend.

1 Dan is in the cab

2 The cat is in the cab

3 Mom is in the cab

4 We see Dan and Mom

▶ Read the words. Write each word at the end of the correct sentence.

| van.   red. |

5 We can go in the _____

6 The van is _____

Periods

▶ Read each group of words. Fill in the
circle next to the correct sentence.

1

◯ The cat is on the mat.

◯ the cat is on the mat

◯ the cat on the mat

2

◯ the rat is on the mop

◯ the rat is on the mop

◯ The rat is on the mop.

3

◯ The rat sees the cat

◯ The rat sees the cat.

◯ the rat sees the cat

4

◯ The rat can hop.

◯ The rat can hop

◯ the rat can hop

5

◯ the cat and rat sit

◯ The cat and rat sit

◯ The cat and rat sit.

Capitalizing I

Always write the word I with a capital letter.

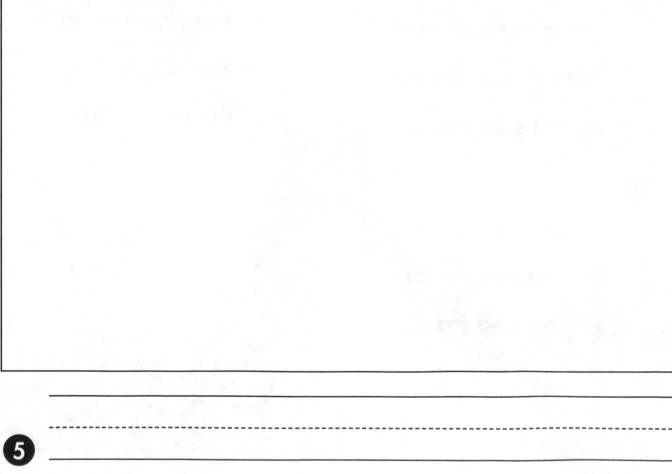

▶ Circle the word I in each sentence.

1 I like to hop.

2 Pam and I like to hop.

3 I can hop to Mom.

4 Mom and I can hop.

▶ Draw what you like. Use the word I to write about it.

5 _____

Capitalizing I

Always write the word I with a capital letter.

▶ Read the sentences. Write I on the line.

1 _____ will ride.

2 _____ will swim.

3 Mom and _____ will sing.

4 Then _____ will read.

▶ What will you do next? Write it on the line.

5 I will

Capitalizing **I**

▶ Read each group of words. Fill in
the circle next to the correct sentence.

1
- ◯ i sit on a mat.
- ◯ I sit on a mat.
- ◯ i sit on a mat

2
- ◯ Pam and I like cats.
- ◯ Pam and i like cats.
- ◯ pam and i like cats

3
- ◯ I see the van.
- ◯ i see the van.
- ◯ i see the van

4
- ◯ i like jam.
- ◯ i like jam
- ◯ I like jam.

5
- ◯ i like to nap.
- ◯ I like to nap.
- ◯ i like to nap

Simple Sentences

A sentence tells a complete idea.

 Circle who or what each sentence is about.

1 Pam ran.

2 Dan hops.

3 The cat sits.

4 The van can go.

 Draw a line from each sentence to the picture of who or what the sentence is about.

5 Jan is hot.

6 The hat is on top.

7 The man sat.

Simple Sentences

A sentence tells a complete idea.

▶ Circle each sentence.

1 Bill
Bill paints.

2 likes to read
Tom likes to read.

3 plants flowers
Pat plants flowers.

▶ Finish the sentence.

4 I like

Simple Sentences

▶ Read each group of words. Fill in the circle next to the complete sentence.

1

◯ on a mat

◯ The cat sits on a mat.

◯ The cat

2

◯ Pam and Dan like jam.

◯ Pam and Dan

◯ like jam

3

◯ I see Mom.

◯ I see

◯ Mom

4

◯ my hat

◯ I like

◯ I like my hat.

5

◯ Ben.

◯ Ben can hop.

◯ hop

Word Order

Words in a sentence must be in an order that makes sense.

▶ Read each group of words. Draw a line under the word that should go first in each sentence.

1 dots. I like

2 Pam dots. likes

3 like We hats.

4 hats with dots. We like

▶ Now write each group of words in the right order.

1 _____

_____

2 _____

_____

3 _____

_____

4 _____

Word Order

Words in a sentence must be in an order that makes sense.

▶ Read each group of words. Write them in the right order on the lines.

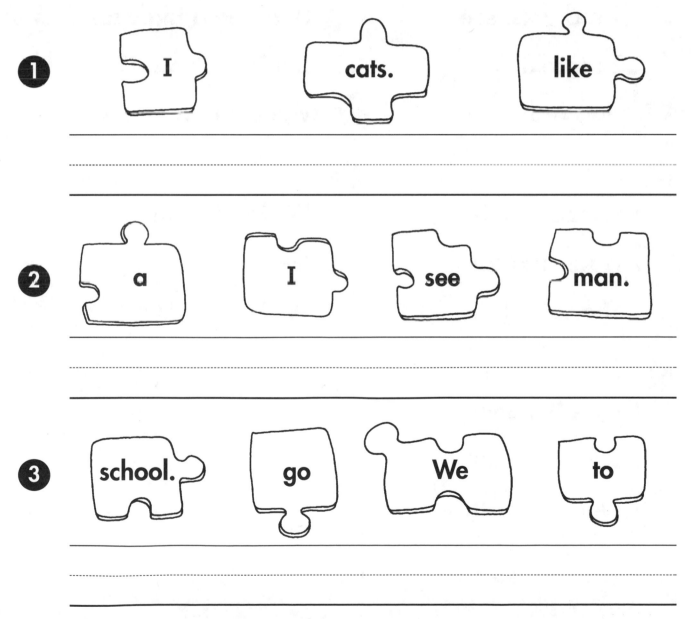

1 I cats. like

_____

2 a I see man.

_____

3 school. go We to

_____

To the Teacher: Remind children that a sentence begins with a capital letter. Point out that a telling sentence ends with a period.

Word Order

▶ Read each group of words. Fill in the circle next to the words that are in an order that makes sense.

1
- ○ I red dots. see
- ○ I see red dots.
- ○ dots red

2
- ○ Dan is in a big van.
- ○ big Dan a van. is in
- ○ van big Dan in a is

3
- ○ fat. cat The is
- ○ is fat. The cat
- ○ The cat is fat.

4
- ○ We like the hat.
- ○ the like hat. We
- ○ We hat. the like

5
- ○ likes Ben jam.
- ○ Ben likes jam.
- ○ jam. likes Ben

Question Sentences

Question sentences ask something.

 Read each sentence. Circle each
question mark.

1 Who hid the hat?

2 Is it on the cat?

3 Can you see the hat?

4 Is it on the man?

 Write two questions. Draw a line under
each capital letter at the beginning of
each question. Circle the question marks.

5 _____

_____

6 _____

_____

Question Sentences

Question sentences ask something.

 Draw a line under each sentence that asks a question. Circle the question mark.

1 Who hid the cat?

2 Can the cat see the rat?

3 The cat is in the van.

4 Can the van go?

 Read the sentences. Circle each sentence that asks something.

5 Can we sit in the van?

We can sit in the van.

6 Dan can nap in the van.

Can Dan nap in the van?

Question Sentences

▶ Read the sentences. Fill in the circle
next to the sentence that asks a question.

1

- ○ Who hid my hat?
- ○ My hat is with him.
- ○ My hat is big.

2

- ○ The hat has spots.
- ○ The hat has dots.
- ○ Did the hat have dots?

3

- ○ Jan likes my hat.
- ○ Did Jan like my hat?
- ○ Jan did like my hat.

4

- ○ Can you see the hat?
- ○ You can see the hat.
- ○ She can see the hat.

5

- ○ Dan can get a hat.
- ○ Dan likes hats.
- ○ Dan has the hat?

Naming Words

A naming word names a person, place, or thing.

 Read each sentence. Draw a line under the word or words that name the person, place, or thing in each sentence.

1 **The pig is big.**

2 **The pan is hot.**

3 **Pam hid.**

4 **Can you run up the hill?**

 Draw a line from each sentence to the picture that shows the naming word in that sentence.

5 **The sun is hot.**

6 **Sam ran and ran.**

7 **Is the cat fat?**

Naming Words

A naming word names a person, place, or thing.

▶ Circle the naming words in the sentences.

1 Al can go in a van.

2 The cat sat on a mat.

3 Pat ran up the hill.

4 Dan and Jan will mop.

▶ Draw a picture of a person, place, or thing. Write a sentence about your picture. Circle the naming word.

5

Naming Words

▶ Read each sentence. Fill in the circle next to the naming word.

1 I see a big cat.

    (a) **see**   (b) **big**   (c) **cat**

2 The rat ran fast.

    (a) **ran**   (b) **rat**   (c) **fast**

3 Can you see the map?

    (a) **Can**   (b) **map**   (c) **see**

4 The van is tan.

    (a) **van**   (b) **is**   (c) **tan**

5 The fan is not on!

    (a) **not**   (b) **on**   (c) **fan**

Capitalize Special Names

The names of people, places, and pets are special.
They begin with capital letters.

 Draw a line under the special name in
each sentence. Then circle the first letter
or letters in that name.

1 They go to Hill Park.

2 Pam sees the ham.

3 Don sees the cat.

4 They like Frog Lake.

 Write a special name of a person, place, or pet
you know.

_____

- -

5 _____

Capitalize Special Names

The names of people, places, and pets are special. They begin with capital letters.

▶ Circle each special name. Draw a line under each capital letter in each name.

 I am Pam.

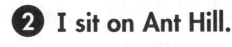 I sit on Ant Hill.

3 Ron likes the lake.

4 He likes Bat Lake.

▶ Read the special names in the box.
Write a special name for each picture.

Spot   Hill Street

5 _____

- - - - - - - - - - - - - - - - - - - -

_____

6 _____

- - - - - - - - - - - - - - - - - - - -

_____

Capitalize Special Names

▶ Read each sentence. Fill in the circle next to the special name.

1 Can Don go to the picnic?

- ⬭ picnic
- ⬭ Don
- ⬭ Can

2 The picnic will be on Pig Hill.

- ⬭ Pig Hill
- ⬭ picnic
- ⬭ The

3 The hill is on Jam Street.

- ⬭ hill
- ⬭ The
- ⬭ Jam Street

4 Jan will go to the picnic.

- ⬭ go
- ⬭ picnic
- ⬭ Jan

5 She will go in Ham Lake.

- ⬭ She
- ⬭ Ham Lake
- ⬭ will

Action Words

An action word tells what happens.

▶ Read each sentence. Circle the word that tells what happens.

1 The hen sits.

2 The cat ran.

3 Pam hid.

4 The dog naps.

▶ Read the words. Use the words to finish the sentences.

| run | see |

_____
----

5 I will _____ up the hill.

_____
----

6 I _____ a big pig.

Action Words

An action word tells what happens.

▶ Look at each picture. Read the words. Write the action word.

1   I can see.

_____

2   The cat sits.

_____

3   Mom mops.

_____

4   We run fast.

_____

5   It hops a lot.

_____

Action Words

▶ Read each sentence.
Fill in the circle next to the action word.

1 I sit on a hill.

ⓐ I   ⓑ sit   ⓒ hill

2 The rat ran fast.

ⓐ ran   ⓑ rat   ⓒ fast

3 We mop a lot.

ⓐ We   ⓑ lot   ⓒ mop

4 The dog digs up sand.

ⓐ dog   ⓑ sand   ⓒ digs

5 Pam hops up and down.

ⓐ hops   ⓑ up   ⓒ Pam

Describing Words

A describing word tells more about a person, place, or thing.

▶ Read each sentence. Circle the word that tells about the cat.

1 I see a **big** cat.

2 The **fast** cat ran.

3 My cat is **bad**.

4 The **fat** cat naps.

▶ Look at each cat. Circle the word that tells about it.

5

fat　　**little**

6

big　　**little**

Describing Words

A describing word tells more about a person, place, or thing.

▶ Look at each picture. Circle the words that tell about it.

1

big   fast

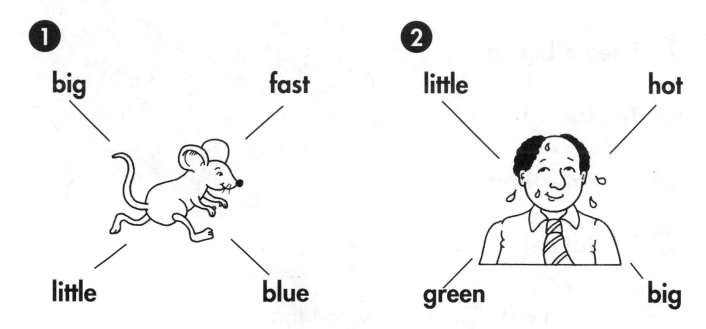

little   blue

2

little   hot

green   big

▶ Draw a line between each sentence and the picture that shows what it describes.

3 It is fat.

4 They are little.

Describing Words

▶ Read each sentence. Fill in the circle
next to the describing word.

1 The silly cat can play.

◯ silly

◯ cat

◯ play

2 The bad rat will run.

◯ bad

◯ run

◯ rat

3 The black dog naps.

◯ dog

◯ black

◯ naps

4 The cow is big.

◯ cow

◯ is

◯ big

5 A green frog can hop.

◯ frog

◯ green

◯ hop

Telling Sentences

A telling sentence tells something.

 Circle the capital letter at the beginning of each telling sentence. Then circle the period at the end of each telling sentence.

1 I see the basket.

2 The cat is in the basket.

3 Hats can go in it.

4 The sock can go in it.

 Draw a line under each telling sentence.

5 I can fill the basket.

6 Can you get the mop?

7 We can clean.

Telling Sentences

A telling sentence tells something.

▶ Draw a line to match each sentence with the picture that shows what the sentence tells.

1 She has a mop.

2 The dog is on top.

3 Dan gets the hats.

4 Ron can clean spots.

▶ Read the sentences. Circle the capital letter and period in the telling sentence.

5 Put it in the pot. **6** Is it in the pan?

Telling Sentences

▶ Read the sentences. Fill in the circle next to each sentence that tells something.

1
- ◯ Can you get the basket?
- ◯ You can get it.
- ◯ Can you fill it?

2
- ◯ The basket is big.
- ◯ Is the basket big?
- ◯ Why is it big?

3
- ◯ What can go in it?
- ◯ Will the hat go in?
- ◯ The hat is in the basket.

4
- ◯ A cat can not go in it.
- ◯ Can a cat go in?
- ◯ Will a cat go in it?

5
- ◯ Can we fill it?
- ◯ We can fill the basket.
- ◯ Will you fill it?

Exclamation Sentences

Exclamatory sentences show strong feelings such as excitement, surprise, or fear. They end with exclamation marks. (!)

▶ Read each sentence. Circle each exclamation mark. Draw a line under the capital letter at the beginning of each sentence.

1 Help! The rat is on top!

2 Get the cat!

3 This cat is bad!

4 Uh-oh! The cat is wet!

▶ Read each set of sentences. Draw a line under the sentence or sentences that show strong feeling.

5 Oh my! Get the dog!

Let's get the dog.

6 The dog runs.

Oh! The dog runs!

Exclamation Sentences

> Exclamatory sentences show strong feeling, such as excitement, surprise, or fear. They end with an exclamation mark. (!)

▶ Choose the sentence in each pair that shows strong feeling. Write it on the line. Put an exclamation mark at the end.

1   Run to the show   We will go to the show

_____

2   I'm late for it   Oh my, I'm very late

_____

3   What a great show   I liked the show

_____

4   The floor is wet   Watch out, the floor is wet

_____

5   We had fun   Wow, we had lots of fun

_____

Exclamation Sentences

▶ Read each group of sentences. Fill in the circle next to the sentence or sentences that show strong feeling.

1
- ◯ The cow is on the hill.
- ◯ The cow likes grass.
- ◯ Yes! The cow can kick!

2
- ◯ That cat is bad!
- ◯ That cat naps.
- ◯ Is the cat on the mat?

3
- ◯ The rat will run.
- ◯ That rat runs fast!
- ◯ The rat can hop.

4
- ◯ Oh no! A frog is in my house!
- ◯ A frog hops.
- ◯ The frog is green.

5
- ◯ The pot can get hot.
- ◯ The pot is hot!
- ◯ Fill the pot with mud.

Singular/Plural Nouns

Many nouns, or naming words, add <u>-s</u> to show more than one.

▶ Read each sentence. Draw a line under each naming word that means more than one.

1 I see hats and a cap.　　**2** It sits on eggs.

3 The girls swim.　　**4** Pam can pet cats.

▶ Read each sentence. Write the naming word that means more than one.

5 The mugs are hot.　　_____

6 Mud is on my hands.　　_____

Singular/Plural Nouns

Many nouns, or naming words, add -s to show more than one.

▶ Read the sets of sentences. Draw a line under the sentence that has a naming word that names more than one.

1 Jan has her mittens.

Jan has her mitten.

2 She will run up a hill.

She will run up hills.

3 Jan runs with her dogs.

Jan runs with her dog.

4 The dogs can jump.

The dog can jump.

▶ Look at each picture. Read each word. Write the plural naming word that matches the picture.

5 _____

cat _____

6 _____

sock _____

Singular/Plural Nouns

▶ Read each sentence. Fill in the circle next to the naming word that means more than one.

1 Jim gets mud on his hands.

- ○ gets
- ○ hands
- ○ mud

2 Pam can fill the pots with mud.

- ○ pots
- ○ mud
- ○ fill

3 The dogs dig fast.

- ○ dig
- ○ fast
- ○ dogs

4 The ants are on the plant.

- ○ ants
- ○ plant
- ○ are

5 The frogs hop.

- ○ The
- ○ frogs
- ○ hop

Action Words

An action word tells what happens.

▶ Read each sentence. Circle the word
that tells what happens.

1 The hen sits.   **2** Mom sees the hen.

3 The dog digs.   **4** The cat naps.

▶ Read the words. Use the words to finish
the sentences.

sees	run

5 She _____ eggs.

6 It can _____ fast.

Action Words

An action word tells what happens.

▶ Look at the pictures. Read the action words in the box. Write the correct action word on the line.

talk
play
dance
run

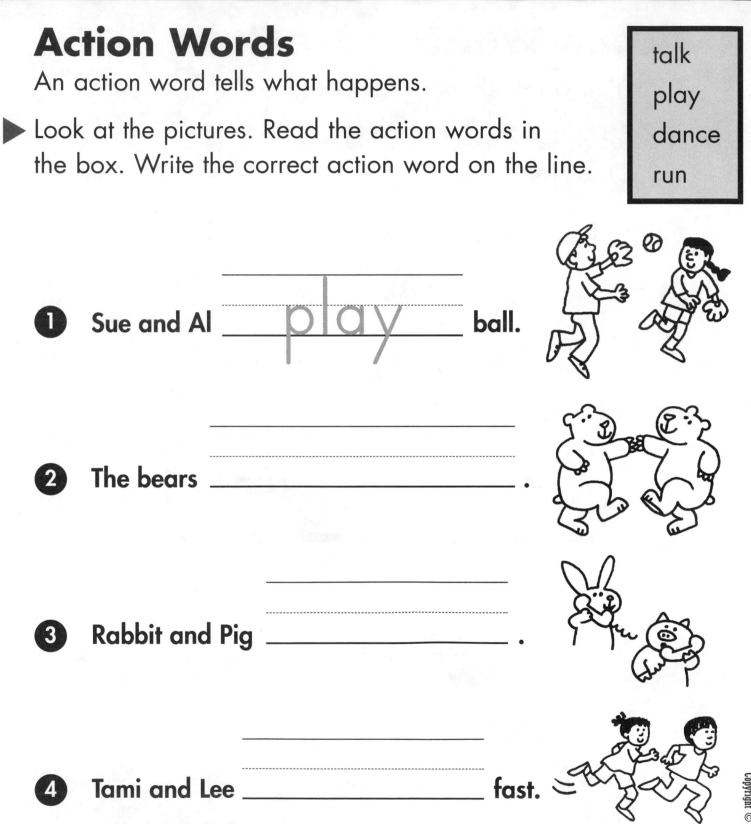

1 Sue and Al _____play_____ ball.

2 The bears _____.

3 Rabbit and Pig _____.

4 Tami and Lee _____ fast.

To the Teacher: Read the words in the box with children. Help children understand that they tell what the characters in the pictures are doing.

Action Words

▶ Read each sentence. Fill in the circle
next to the action word.

1 The hen sits.
- ○ hen
- ○ sits
- ○ The

2 The cat naps in the van.
- ○ naps
- ○ cat
- ○ van

3 The green frog hops.
- ○ frog
- ○ green
- ○ hops

4 The dog digs.
- ○ digs
- ○ dog
- ○ The

5 The big pig ran.
- ○ big
- ○ pig
- ○ ran

Naming Words

A naming word names a person, place, or thing.

▶ Read each sentence. Draw a line under the naming word.

1 We play at school.

2 The ball is fast.

3 The girl kicks.

4 The friends run.

▶ Look at each box. Circle the naming word that belongs in that box.

Person	Place	Thing
girl	ball	Pam
school	Bill	man
ball	school	ball

Naming Words

A naming word names a person, place, or thing.

 Read each sentence. Circle each naming word. Draw a line to match the sentence to the picture of the naming word.

1 Run and kick in the park.

2 Kick with a foot.

3 Kick the ball.

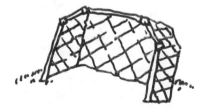

4 The girl will run to get it.

5 Kick it to the net.

Naming Words

▶ Read each sentence. Fill in the circle next to the word that names a person, place, or thing.

1 Let's play in the park.

◯ play

◯ Let's

◯ park

2 The girl can run and kick.

◯ girl

◯ run

◯ kick

3 Kick the ball.

◯ ball

◯ the

◯ kick

4 The friend can jump.

◯ can

◯ jump

◯ friend

5 Jump to the net.

◯ get

◯ net

◯ jump

Word Order

Words in a sentence must be in an order that makes sense.

 Read each group of words. Circle the words that are in an order that makes sense. Draw a line under each capital letter.

1 The king is sad.

sad. king is The

2 bake Let's cake. him a

Let's bake him a cake.

3 the king Tell to come.

Tell the king to come.

4 Let's eat the cake.

eat Let's the cake.

 Read the words. Write them in order.

king The . eats

_____

- -

_____

Word Order

Words in a sentence must be in an order that makes sense.

▶ These words are mixed up. Put them in order. Then write each sentence.

1 snow. bear likes This

_____

- - - - - - - - - - - - - - - - - - -

_____

2 water cold. The is

_____

- - - - - - - - - - - - - - - - - - -

_____

3 fast. The runs bear

_____

- - - - - - - - - - - - - - - - - - -

_____

4 play. bears Two

_____

- - - - - - - - - - - - - - - - - - -

_____

Word Order

► Read each group of words. Then fill in the circle next to the words that are in an order that makes sense.

1
- ○ Pam will bake a cake.
- ○ bake Pam a will cake.
- ○ will Pam cake. a bake

2
- ○ will king. the see Pam
- ○ king. Pam see will the
- ○ Pam will see the king.

3
- ○ duck. The king has a
- ○ The king has a duck.
- ○ has a king The duck.

4
- ○ lake. the in is The duck
- ○ The duck is in the lake.
- ○ The lake. duck in is the

5
- ○ The king will eat cake.
- ○ king will The cake. eat
- ○ cake. king will The eat

Capitalizing Titles

Important words in a title are capitalized.

▶ Circle all the words that are capitalized.

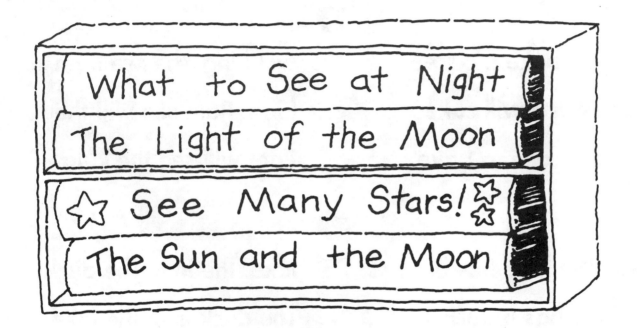

What to See at Night
The Light of the Moon
☆ See Many Stars! ☆
The Sun and the Moon

▶ Now use some of the words from the titles above to write your own titles.

_____

- - - - - - - - - - - - - - - - - - -

_____

- - - - - - - - - - - - - - - - - - -

_____

Capitalizing Titles

Important words in a title are capitalized.

▶ Read the titles. Circle all the words that should be capitalized.

1 look at the stars!

2 the moon shines at night

3 we see planets

4 many moons shine

5 night and day

▶

Read each set of titles. Draw a line under the correct title.

6 The Sun in the Sky

the sun in the sky

7 See the stars!

See the Stars!

Capitalizing Titles

▶ Read the titles. Fill in the circle next to the title with the correct words capitalized.

1

⬭ **Where Is the Sun?**

⬭ **Where is the sun?**

⬭ **Where Is The Sun?**

2

⬭ **many cats to see**

⬭ **Many cats To See**

⬭ **Many Cats to See**

3

⬭ **Day and Night**

⬭ **day And night**

⬭ **Day And Night**

4

⬭ **how many pigs?**

⬭ **How Many Pigs?**

⬭ **How many pigs?**

5

⬭ **the Big Bad wolf**

⬭ **the big, bad wolf**

⬭ **The Big, Bad Wolf**

Naming Words

A naming word names a person, place, or thing.

▶ Read each sentence. Draw a line under the word or words that name the person, place, or thing in each sentence.

1 The pot is big.   **2** The pan is big.

3 See the top?   **4** Jim can mop.

▶ Draw a line from each sentence to the picture that shows the naming word in that sentence.

5 The pot is hot.

6 See the pan?

7 Jim is fast.

Naming Words

A naming word names a person, place, or thing.

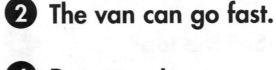

 Circle the naming words in the sentences.

1 Jan can go in a van.　　**2** The van can go fast.

3 The van is on a hill.　　**4** Dan sees Jan.

 Draw a picture of a person, place, or thing.
Write a sentence about your picture.
Circle the naming word.

5

Naming Words

▶ Read each sentence. Fill in the circle next to the naming word.

1 See the hot pans?

○ hot

○ See

○ pans

2 See Jim mop fast.

○ fast

○ Jim

○ See

3 The cat naps.

○ cat

○ The

○ naps

4 The rat hid.

○ The

○ rat

○ hid

5 Can the cat see?

○ see

○ cat

○ Can

Linking Verbs

Is, are, was, and were are linking verbs. Is tells about one. Are tells about more than one. Was tells about one in the past. Were tells about more than one in the past.

▶ Read each sentence. Draw a line under the linking verb is, are, was, or were.

1 The hen is digging.

2 The chicks were helping.

3 The pig was having fun.

4 The cat and duck are playing.

▶ Read each sentence. Circle now or in the past to show when it happens or happened.

5 The hen is planting.   now   in the past

6 The cat was not helping.   now   in the past

7 The chicks are with the hen.   now   in the past

Linking Verbs

Is, are, was, and were are linking verbs. Is tells about one. Are tells about more than one. Was tells about one in the past. Were tells about more than one in the past.

▶ Circle the linking verb. Write now or past to tell when the action happens or happened.

_____

1 The chicks are eating. _____

2 The duck is swimming. _____

3 The cat was napping. _____

4 The pig is digging. _____

5 They were playing. _____

Linking Verbs

▶ Fill in the circle next to the linking verb that completes each sentence.

1 The hen ___ sitting.
- ⬭ was
- ⬭ are
- ⬭ were

2 They ___ playing.
- ⬭ were
- ⬭ is
- ⬭ was

3 The pigs ___ digging.
- ⬭ was
- ⬭ is
- ⬭ are

4 The duck ___ swimming.
- ⬭ were
- ⬭ is
- ⬭ are

5 The chicks ___ napping.
- ⬭ was
- ⬭ is
- ⬭ are

Capitalizing Names and First Words

The first word in a sentence starts with a capital letter. Sometimes words that name a person, place, or thing begin with a capital letter.

▶ Read the sentences. Circle the words that are capitalized.

1 The goats Gruff have a problem.

2 They do not like the Troll.

3 His name is Nosey.

4 He is big and bad.

▶ Draw a line to match each sentence to why the underlined word is capitalized.

5 Dan and <u>Pam</u> like the play.   First word in a sentence.

6 <u>They</u> will read it to Jim.   Names a person, place, or thing.

Capitalizing Names

Sometimes the names of people, places, and things are special. They begin with a capital letter.

▶ Circle the special names in the picture. Write each one correctly on a line.

1 _____

2 _____

3 _____

4 _____

Capitalizing Names and First Words

 Read each sentence. Fill in the circle next to the word that needs a capital letter.

1 i like the goats Gruff.

◯ Goats

◯ The

◯ I

2 I read the story with ron.

◯ Read

◯ Story

◯ Ron

3 Little gruff had a problem.

◯ Had

◯ Gruff

◯ Problem

4 troll was on the bridge.

◯ A

◯ Bridge

◯ Troll

5 His name was nosey.

◯ Name

◯ Nosey

◯ His

Answer Key

Page 4
1. The 2. The 3. The 4. The

Page 5
1. The cat sat. 3. I see the cat.
2. The dog sat. 4. I can see.

Page 6
1. The 3. Jan 5. Ants
2. My 4. I

Page 7
1. I see Jan○
2. I go with Jan○
3. We see Dan○
4. I go with Dan and Jan○
5. school.
6. school.

Page 8
1. Dan is in the cab.
2. The cat is in the cab.
3. Mom is in the cab.
4. We see Dan and Mom.
5. van.
6. red.

Page 9
1. The cat is on the mat.
2. The rat is on the mop.
3. The rat sees the cat.
4. The rat can hop.
5. The cat and rat sit.

Page 10
1. ⓘ like to hop.
2. Pam and ⓘ like to hop.
3. ⓘ can hop to Mom.
4. Mom and ⓘ can hop.
5. Answers will vary.

Page 11
1. I 4. I
2. I 5. answers will vary
3. I

Page 12
1. I sit on a mat.
2. Pam and I like cats.
3. I see the van.
4. I like jam.
5. I like to nap.

Page 13
1. Pam 3. The cat
2. Dan 4. The van
5. Jan is hot. ———
6. The hat is on top. ———
7. The man sat. ———

Page 14
1. Bill paints.
2. Tom likes to read.
3. Pat plants flowers.
4. answers will vary

Page 15
1. The cat sits on a mat.
2. Pam and Dan like jam.
3. I see Mom.
4. I like my hat.
5. Ben can hop.

Page 16
1. I
2. Pam
3. We
4. We
1. I like dots.
2. Pam likes dots.
3. We like hats.
4. We like hats with dots.

Page 17
1. I like cats.
2. I see a man.
3. We go to school

Page 18
1. I see red dots.
2. Dan is in a big van.
3. The cat is fat.
4. We like the hat.
5. Ben likes jam.

Page 19
1. ⓠ 4. ⓠ
2. ⓠ 5. Answers will vary.
3. ⓠ 6. Answers will vary.

Page 20
1. Who hid the cat⓪
2. Can the cat see the rat⓪
4. Can the van go⓪
5. Can we sit in the van?
6. Can Dan nap in the van?

Page 21
1. Who hid my hat?
2. Did the hat have dots?
3. Did Jan like my hat?
4. Can you see the hat?
5. Dan has the hat?

Page 22
1. pig 3. Pam
2. pan 4. hill
5. The sun is hot. ———
6. Sam ran and ran. ———
7. Is the cat fat? ———

Page 23
1. Al, van 3. Pat, hill
2. cat, mat 4. Dan, Jan

Page 24
1. c. 2. b 3. b 4. a 5. c

Page 25
1. Ⓗill Ⓟark 4. Ⓕrog Ⓛake
2. Ⓟam 5. Answers will vary
3. Ⓓon

Page 26
1. Pam. 4. Bat Lake
2. Ant Hill. 5. Spot
3. Ron 6. Hill Street

Page 27
1. Don 4. Jan
2. Pig Hill 5. Ham Lake
3. Jam Street

Page 28
1. sits 3. hid 5. run
2. ran 4. naps 6. see

Page 29
1. see 3. mops 5. hops
2. sits 4. run

Page 30
1. b 2. a 3. c 4. c 5. a

Page 31
1. big 3. bad 5. fat
2. fast 4. fat 6. little

Page 32
1. little, fast
2. hot, big
3. It is fat.
4. They are little.

Page 33
1. silly 3. black 5. green
2. bad 4. big

Page 34
1. I,
2. T,
3. H,
4. T,
5. I can fill the basket.
6. Can you get the mop?
7. We can clean.

Page 35
1. She has a mop. ———
2. The dog is on top. ———
3. Dan gets the hats. ———
4. Ron can clean spots. ———
5. Ⓟut it in the pot ○
6. Is it in the pan?

Page 36
1. You can get it.
2. The basket is big.
3. The hat is in the basket.
4. A cat can not go in it.
5. We can fill the basket.

Page 37
1. Help⓵ The rat is on top⓵
2. Get the cat⓵
3. This cat is bad⓵
4. Uh-oh⓵ The cat is wet⓵
5. Oh my⓵ Get the dog⓵
6. Oh⓵ The dog runs⓵

Page 38
1. Run to the show!
2. Oh my, I'm very late!
3. What a great show!
4. Watch out, the floor is wet!
5. Wow, we had lots of fun!

Page 39
1. Yes! The cow can kick!
2. That cat is bad!
3. That rat runs fast!
4. Oh no! A frog is in my house!
5. The pot is hot!

Page 40
1. hats 3. girls 5. mugs
2. eggs 4. cats 6. hands

Page 41
1. Jan has her mittens.
2. She will run up hills.
3. Jan runs with her dogs.
4. The dogs can jump.
5. cats
6. socks

Page 42
1. hands 3. dogs 5. frogs
2. pots 4. ants

Page 43
1. sits 3. digs 5. sees
2. sees 4. naps 6. run

Page 44
1. play 3. talk
2. dance 4. run

Page 45
1. sits 3. hops 5. ran
2. naps 4. digs

page 46
1. school
2. ball
3. girl
4. friends
Person: girl
Place: school
Thing: ball

Page 47
1. Run and kick ——— in the park.
2. Kick with a foot. ———
3. Kick the ball. ———
4. The girl will run ——— to get it.
5. Kick it to the net. ———

Page 48
1. park 3. ball 5. net
2. girl 4. friend

Page 49
1. The king is sad.
2. Let's bake him a cake.
3. Tell the king to come.
4. Let's eat the cake.
The king eats.

Page 50
1. This bear likes snow.
2. The water is cold.
3. The bear runs fast.
4. Two bears play.

Page 51
1. Pam will bake a cake.
2. Pam will see the king.
3. The king has a duck.
4. The duck is in the lake.
5. The king will eat cake.

Page 52
circle: What, See, Night, The, Light, Moon, See, Many, Stars, The, Sun, Moon
Answers will vary.

Page 53
1. look, stars
2. the, moon, shines, night
3. we, see, planets
4. many, moons, shine
5. night, day
6. The Sun in the Sky
7. See the Stars!

Page 54
1. Where is the Sun?
2. Many Cats to See
3. Day and Night
4. How Many Pigs?
5. The Big, Bad Wolf

Page 55
1. pot
2. pan
3. top
4. Jim
5. The pot is hot. ———
6. See the pan? ———
7. Jim is fast. ———

Page 56
1. Jan, van
2. van
3. van, hill
4. Dan, Jan
5. answers will vary

Page 57
1. pans 3. cat 5. cat
2. Jim 4. rat

Page 58
1. is 5. now
2. were 6. in the past
3. was 7. now
4. are

Page 59
1. are, now 4. is, now
2. is, now 5. were, past
3. was, past

Page 60
1. was 3. are 5. are
2. were 4. is

Page 61
1. The, Gruff
2. They, Troll
3. His, Nosey
4. He
5. Dan and Pam like the play.
Names a person, place, or thing.
6. They will read it to Jim.
First word in a sentence.

Page 62
1. Raul 3. Sue
2. Mrs. Chin 4. Lee Park

Page 63
1. I 3. Gruff 5. Nosey
2. Ron 4. Troll